GIANTS of RAP and HIP-HOP

J. COLE

Bradley Steffens

ReferencePoint
Press

San Diego, CA

About the Author

Bradley Steffens is a poet, a novelist, and an award-winning author of more than fifty nonfiction books for children and young adults.

For more information, contact:
ReferencePoint Press, Inc.
PO Box 27779
San Diego, CA 92198
www.ReferencePointPress.com

Picture Credits:

Cover: Daniel DeSlover/Zuma Press/Newscom

 5: Associated Press
 9: Associated Press
12: Watch the World/Shutterstock.com
15: associated Press
19: Luciano Mortula/Shutterstock.com
21: Photofest
25: AB1/Adriana M. Barraza/WENN/Newscom

30: PN2/ARB/PNP/WENN/Newscom
33: Charlie Bryan/Retna Pictures/Photoshot/
     Newscom
38: William Howard/Icon Sportswire/DJF
40: Goldilock Project/Shutterstock.com
43: IB2/WENN/Newscom
48: Iakov Filimonov/Shutterstock.com
50: Associated Press
53: Ricky Bassman/Cal Sport Media/Newscom

LIBRARY OF CONGRESS CATALOGING-IN-PUBLICATION DATA

Names: Steffens, Bradley, 1955– author.
Title: J. Cole/by Bradley Steffens.
Description: San Diego: ReferencePoint Press, 2019. | Series: Giants of
    Rap and Hip-Hop | Includes bibliographical references and index. |
    Audience: Grades 10–12
Identifiers: LCCN 2019031779 (print) | LCCN 2019031780 (ebook) | ISBN
    9781682827772 (library binding) | ISBN 9781682827789 (ebook)
Subjects: LCSH: Cole, J. (Jermaine), 1985—Juvenile literature. | Rap
    musicians—United States—Biography—Juvenile literature.
Classification: LCC ML3930.C5286 S74 2019 (print) | LCC ML3930.C5286
    (ebook) | DDC 782.421649092 [B]—dc23
LC record available at https://lccn.loc.gov/2019031779
LC ebook record available at https://lccn.loc.gov/2019031780

CONTENTS

VOICE OF THE COMMUNITY

Raleigh, North Carolina, had never seen anything quite like it. On April 6, 2019, some of the biggest names in hip-hop music appeared together at an outdoor concert in the city's historic Dorothea Dix Park. More than forty thousand people attended the sold-out show, making it the largest concert in Raleigh's history. The program included a mix of local musicians and national acts, including Big Sean, 21 Savage, Saba, Teyana Taylor, 6LACK, and Nelly. The last artist to perform, the event's headliner, was J. Cole, the record-breaking rapper whose first five albums all went to number one on the *Billboard* 200 chart and whose most recent album, *KOD*, had broken the record for most album streams in one day on both Spotify and Apple Music. *KOD* had also debuted at number one in five different countries and in the top ten of eight more.

Rapper with a Cause

Cole was more than the Raleigh concert's headliner. He was its organizer. And the concert was not staged to enrich its stars. Its profits were donated to the Dorothea Dix Park Conservancy, a nonprofit organization that maintains the park, and to the Dreamville Foundation, a nonprofit organization with the goal of helping provide better futures for urban youth in Fayetteville, North Carolina, Cole's hometown. The Dreamville Foundation was founded in 2011 by none other than J. Cole himself.

Cole's concern for the less fortunate is not isolated to a few benefit concerts. It permeates his work. He raps about the struggles of growing up as the mixed-race son of a white single mom and an African American US Army soldier. He discusses the rift between his parents and the pain of growing up without his father in his life. He talks about the challenges of leaving Fayetteville for college in New York and eventually a career in music. His songs explore concerns in the African American community, including mass incarceration, racial discrimination, gang violence, drug addiction, and depression.

At a time when many rappers sing about their wealth and fame, Cole turns those boasts into questions. Why do some people have so much and others have so little? What role do drugs play in the direction a person's life takes? What about skin color? How does it affect everyday life in America? "We're still Black Americans. Those mental chains are still in us," Cole told Colorlines, an online magazine. "That brainwashing that tells us that light skin is better, it's subconsciously in us, whether we know it or not. . . . I might not be as successful as I am now if I was dark skin."[1]

"We're still Black Americans. Those mental chains are still in us."[1]

—J. Cole

Rapper J. Cole performs during the halftime show at the National Basketball Association All-Star basketball game in Charlotte, North Carolina, in February 2019.

Creating Alter Egos

Cole asks these difficult questions in a variety of ways. In his 2016 album, *4 Your Eyez Only*, Cole raps not as himself but from the point of view of a young man who goes from selling drugs to falling in love and starting a family. By adopting a fictional voice, Cole is able to explore issues of economic hardship, the drug culture, and social inequality in a down-to-earth way that speaking in his own voice as a rap star would not allow him to do.

On *KOD*, Cole raps as kiLL Edward, who is listed on the album's liner notes as a guest artist. "The name [J. Cole] started to feel like a box," he says of using the alias. "I was like 'Yo, I don't wanna talk about myself no more.'" He says he took the name Edward from his stepfather, a man whose influence he wants to "kill." Cole says, "There's aspects of myself . . . that I want to overcome and beat, that I got from him."[2] In 2018 Cole told the online music and culture publication Fader that he was working on a full-length kiLL Edward album as a way of exploring painful issues from his past and showing that they can be overcome.

Cole's probing intelligence gives his work a substance that sets him apart from other rappers and keeps listeners engaged as they play his works over and over. "Cole has emerged this decade as one of the US's finest rappers," writes Sam Moore of New Musical Express, a British music website. "He's a confident lyricist with an ear for a hip-pop hook, a willingness to address difficult subjects and an ability to weave compelling stories through his music."[3]

Most critics believe that Cole has grown artistically with each album he has released. As a result, the expectations for his next works are high. Everything about his career so far suggests that Cole is more than capable of meeting and even exceeding those expectations.

CHAPTER ONE

ACADEMIC ACHIEVER

Jermaine Lamarr Cole was born on January 28, 1985, at the US Army Ninety-Seventh General Hospital in Frankfurt, West Germany. His father is an African American US Army veteran who was stationed in Germany when Jermaine was born. His mother, Kay Francis Cole, is also an army veteran. She left the service after giving birth to Jermaine's older brother, Zachary James Cole, or Zach.

Broken Families

When Jermaine was eight months old and Zach was four, their parents separated. Kay took Jermaine and Zach to Fayetteville, North Carolina. At first they lived in military housing, but when Jermaine's parents divorced, the family had to find a new place to live. A postal worker, Kay could only afford low-cost housing. She rented a trailer in a poor part of Fayetteville. "I started off on a military base and I remember moving," says J. Cole. "I guess this is after my parents got divorced, but I remember moving from there straight to a trailer park. And it was, like, one of the scariest places I've been to because I was always worried about my mother."[4] Times were tough, financially. "There were days when my mom would have to scrape up nickels and dimes to give me $1.50 lunch money," Cole recalls. "And I would know she wasn't eating lunch that day so that I could."[5]

By the time Cole was eleven, his mother had remarried, and the family could afford a nicer home. They moved into a single-family home on Forest Hills Drive, a tree-lined street with a creek nearby. For the first time in his young life, Cole had his own bedroom, which was a blessing in many ways. It was a place to listen to music, daydream, and do his homework in private. It also was a haven from his stepfather. "We had this condescending stepfather figure who was really negative," Cole remembers. "There was no love, no connection there. He was physically abusive to us and verbally abusive too, even more so to my brother."[6]

The boys rarely saw their biological father. Cole would later explore the impact his parents' breakup had on him. In the song "Breakdown," he says that when he did see his father after several years of separation, he cried. As he told National Public Radio, "It just felt so good to see my pops. . . . It was one of those breakdown moments."[7]

Questions of Color

The son of a black man and a white woman, Cole has given a lot of thought to his biracial heritage. He does not look a lot like his mother or brother. His mother has green eyes, red hair, and freckled skin; his brother has blue eyes, blond hair, and pale skin; and Cole has brown eyes, black hair, and light brown skin. Cole says he identifies more strongly with being black, mainly because that is how others see him. He says:

> I can identify with White people, because I know my mother, her side of the family, who I love. . . . But at the end of the day, I never felt White. I don't know what that feels like. I can identify. But never have I felt like I'm one of them. Not that I wanted to, or tried to, but it just was what it was. I identify more with what I look like, because that's how I got treated. Not necessarily in a negative way.[8]

One of Cole's gifts is his ability to see the humor in life. This even extends to serious issues such as race relations. Regarding his biracial status, he jokes, "When you get pulled over by the police, I can't pull out my half-White card.

"I never felt White. I don't know what that feels like. I can identify. But never have I felt like I'm one of them."[8]

—J. Cole

8

Or if I just meet you on the street, you're not gonna be like, 'This guy seems half-White.'"[9]

Cole believes his biracial heritage has benefited him as an artist, allowing him to empathize with both blacks and whites. This gives him the ability to explore social issues without preconceptions or bias. "I'm half black, half white. So, basically, put it like this, I could fit in anywhere," he says. "That's why I write so many stories from so many different perspectives because I've seen so many."[10]

Competitive Drive

Cole's race did not affect him as a student, according to an interview he gave to Lee Hawkins of the *Wall Street Journal*. Citing a 2006 study by a Harvard University economist entitled

Cole Makes His Recording Debut

When J. Cole began producing and rapping with Bomm Sheltuh, the duo was working on a compilation album called *Fayettenam Bommuhs Volume 1*. Nervous Reck and FilthE Ritch recruited the best local talent available for their album. Marcus "Snipes" Womble, founding member of a rap group called Da Wolfpack, teamed up with Nervous Reck and rapper Bigg Mike on a song titled "Terra Firma." Blaque Watch, a street rapper from Fayetteville, contributed a song called "Nothing," which went on to be the biggest record of his career. Nervous Reck and FilthE Ritch also invited J. Cole, rapping as Therapist, to contribute a track to the album. At age sixteen, Cole earned his first liner note credits on a professional recording. In a sign of things to come, Cole's song, "The Storm," a tale of love and betrayal, was the darkest and most introspective song on the twenty-two track project.

"Acting White: The Social Price Paid by the Best and the Brightest Minority Students," Hawkins asked Cole if he had ever been criticized for being a good student. Cole said no, he had not, but that he had seen such criticism directed toward other students and, regrettably, might have even participated in it as a kid. As for himself, he excelled as a student. He says he was always competitive about his grades. When he was in first grade, he constantly asked his teacher what his grade point average was. He recalls, "The teacher would be like, 'Man, you're in the first grade! Why do you want your average?' But it was a competition for me—like, I really want to be the best. Anything I do, I want to do it well."[11]

Cole's drive to excel carried over into his extracurricular activities. Like many kids, he loved basketball. Cole would later title his mixtapes and albums after basketball terminology, including *The Come Up*, *The Warm Up*, and *The Sideline Story*. Cole had ambitions of being a basketball star, but he believes certain factors held him back. "I was always in love with basketball as a kid, but

I thought I was way better than I really was, because I didn't have a male figure around to show me how to actually play," Cole told *Sports Illustrated*. "Me and my brother just kind of figured it out playing rec ball. I went to a middle school that didn't have a team. That kind of set me back."[12]

Cole tried out for the varsity basketball team at Terry Sanford High School as a freshman, but he failed to make the team. He did not take the disappointment well. "I couldn't understand because I thought I was really good, so I blamed the coaches and thought they had it out for me,"[13] he recalls. Instead of giving up, he tried out again as a sophomore, but he was cut again. In what would become an important pattern in his life, his failure inspired self-reflection and ultimately change. He explains:

> I went out the next year and I got cut again. And that's when I really had to take an honest look at myself and be like, yo, why did this happen? It's got to be on me now. I can't blame anybody else. That was the first time I started working like a real basketball player: a thousand shots a day, sprints, minute drills, one-on-one full court with the star player on the team, every day, literally, for the entire school year then the entire summer.[14]

When Cole tried out the next year, he made the team. By his senior year, he was a starting forward. "I wasn't the star player, far from it, but my growth was so quick that by the time I was a freshman in college I had the talent of someone that should have at least been on the bench at a D-I [Division I] school,"[15] he says.

Sports were not Cole's only interest. He also liked music. When he was fourteen, he took up the violin. He applied himself to music with the same drive and determination he had shown in his studies and basketball. By the time he was in high school, he was good enough to be the first-chair violinist in his high school

Music students rehearse with their orchestra conductor. Cole began playing violin at age fourteen. His drive and determination to practice helped him become first-chair violinist in his high school orchestra.

orchestra. He credits the experience with giving him a deeper understanding of music. "Just being in an orchestra every day, even though it was just a school thing, it really taught me about music—more than what I knew at the time," says Cole. "I didn't appreciate it. But how to count notes and how to read music and count beats or whatever so I have that background."[16]

A Passion for Rap

The violin was not Cole's only musical interest. He became interested in rap music at age eight, when his stepfather (at the time his mother's boyfriend) returned from the Gulf War and played Tupac Shakur's debut album, *2Pacalypse Now*, a groundbreaking rap album that discusses racism, police brutality, and teen pregnancy in blunt terms. "I was too young to know what he was talkin' about, but it connected," Cole recalls. "That's

"That's the thing about art: it's just true. It's straight. Whatever you feel, even as a seven-year-old kid, eight-year-old kid, I could hear Pac's early albums and feel the truth."[17]

—J. Cole

the thing about art: it's just true. It's straight. Whatever you feel, even as a seven-year-old kid, eight-year-old kid, I could hear Pac's early albums and feel the truth."[17]

Cole became serious about rap at age twelve. He had an older cousin who enjoyed freestyle rapping—making up rhyming verses on the spot with no preparation. Cole tried it and found it rewarding. He recalls:

> Once I started, I got hooked. I fell in love with rap. I knew that that's what I wanted to do. And once I put my mind to something, and I believe, that's one thing my ma gave me was like stupid confidence. . . . And that's how I was with music. I knew that this was my call. I knew that I wanted to do it for the rest of my life. But I quietly planned and plotted and figured out a way that I could make this happen. So how I got my start was just playin' around, and then it turned into a passion.[18]

Cole filled notebooks with his rhymes and covered the walls of his room with lyrics by his favorite rappers, including Eminem, Canibus, and Nas. "I used to just study these," he says. "Like if I was bored, I'm looking at the wall, reading along, just look how they break down their raps."[19] Confident in his work and wanting to succeed right away, Cole reached out to established stars on their websites and message boards, sending them his lyrics and ideas for songs and videos. No one replied.

At about this time, Cole became interested in the way rap recordings were put together. He noticed that when he listened to rap music, his mother and stepfather would recognize some of the sampled music—bits of well-known songs that are recorded and incorporated into tracks of rap music. He became fascinated with the sampling process. "I think the first time I started paying attention to production was around 1997: the year Biggie's second album [*Life After Death*] and Puff Daddy & the Family's album *No Way Out* came out," he says. "Puff's crew [the Hitmen] was sampling all these older songs that my mom would recognize, or my stepfather would call out, so I got into the credits to find out who produced the songs."[20]

Learning to Produce

Cole begged his mother for recording equipment so he could record samples and create raps. Kay supported her son's newfound passion. For Christmas in 2000, she splurged and gave him a $1,300 professional-grade music sampling workstation. The big-ticket gift came with strings attached. Kay told her son that he would have to forgo a birthday present, buy his own clothes for the next year, and pay for basketball camp with his own money. He agreed. To live up to his financial obligations, Cole took various odd jobs. One of his jobs was to perform as Roller Roo, the mascot of a local roller-skating rink. Cole dressed up in a kangaroo costume, skated around with the kids, and made appearances at birthday parties held in the rink. Although he needed the money, he told MTV that he felt silly in the role: "I felt like less of a man in the kangaroo costume."[21]

This computerized device that his mother gave him had many of the features a professional rap producer needed. It included a digital recording system to record samples of songs by well-known singers and rappers. The user could play a favorite track and then save a digital copy of a section of that recording. Cole went through his mother's CDs, listening for things to sample from a diverse collection of artists, including Steely Dan, Elton John, Eric Clapton, Bob Marley, and Marvin Gaye. The equipment also included a sequencer to stitch those samples together to a timed beat, so the user could make a track-length recording out of the samples. It also had a drum machine so the user could create new rhythms, or "beats," and add them to the tracks.

Later, Cole upgraded his equipment to Reason, a digital audio workstation developed by Propellerhead Software. This system

One of Cole's favorite rappers in his youth was Eminem, pictured here performing at the Bonnaroo Music and Arts Festival in Manchester, Tennessee, in 2018.

included a keyboard and a music synthesizer, so he could create melodies on a keyboard and make them sound like they came from any instrument he chose. "I fell in love with all these instruments," he remembers. "I could make a beat the same way, but then I could pull up a piano on top and play some keys, then go through all these bass lines to choose the one I want. Getting to touch the keys and play changed the whole thing."[22] Equipped with this electronic hardware, Cole began to create his own rap tracks, rapping under the name Blaza.

Turning Pro

After honing his production skills, Cole teamed up with local rappers Nervous Reck and FilthE Ritch, who had formed the group

Cole's Bedroom on Forest Hills Drive

In 2014 J. Cole purchased the house on Forest Hills Drive where he had lived as a child. Cole took a video crew on a tour of the house and discussed the importance of having his own bedroom:

> When we got here, it gave me the ability to close the door. When I got my own room, I could do things like zone out to the music I wanted to hear. I could do things like rap in front of the mirror, and nobody's looking, and I don't feel crazy. I could do things like sit in my own thoughts and write my raps. And that's when I became way more introspective. This is where I started dreaming the dream. . . .
>
> All that [stuff] on TV, that's temporary. The love was important. The love I have for the music. The love I have for rappin'. The love I had when I made my very first song, and that feeling I got—that was important. The love that was in this house, amongst my family, my brother, my mother, the people that really love you, their forever, authentic love is in places like this.

Quoted in Complex, "J. Cole Gives Us a Tour of 2014 Forest Hills Drive in Fayetteville, N.C.," Facebook, January 28, 2018. www.facebook.com.

Bomm Sheltuh. Cole produced Bomm Sheltuh's recordings and sometimes rapped with the group, earning his first money as a musician.

His bandmates did not like the name Blaza, so they encouraged Cole to change it. "We used to look through the dictionary for rap names," he remembers. "I could never find nothing. One day these dudes [in Bomm Sheltuh] were like, 'Yo, we got a name for you, it's Therapist.'" The idea was that Cole would build up a stage image of being a doctor whose music is therapeutic. Cole adopted the moniker, but he eventually tired of the stage persona.

"A few years later, I realized Therapist sounded like a wrestler's name," he says. "You know, like an alias. It didn't feel real." As a result, he dropped Therapist and began calling himself J. Cole—the name he continues to use today. "J. Cole felt like my real name," he says. "That was a real natural fit. It didn't feel like I was trying to be anything."[23]

In the spring of 2003, Cole graduated from high school. He had taken several advanced placement classes, enabling him to graduate with a 4.2 grade point average. His outstanding grades and varsity sports involvement meant that he would likely be accepted at almost any college he applied to. He knew that the University of North Carolina at Chapel Hill had won four National Collegiate Athletic Association basketball championships, including one when he was eight years old. He gave a lot of thought to applying there, but basketball was not his main interest; music was. As much as he loved North Carolina, he knew it was no place to start a career as a rapper. When it was time to apply for college, he set his sights elsewhere.

COMMUNICATIONS MAJOR

When it came time to pick a college, the school's location was of prime importance to J. Cole. He wanted to be in or near a city associated with the music industry. Cole explains:

> This was before this day and age. In this day and age, you can make it from wherever. As long as you have a computer and some great music, you can find people. Back then—this was '03 when I decided to go to school—people weren't blowing up on the Internet. So I was like, "I'm not gonna do it from here. From Fayetteville, North Carolina? It can't happen. Nobody's lookin' here. Nobody's comin' here. And even if I go to Chapel Hill—which I almost went to UNC Chapel Hill—nobody's comin' there, either. Let me go to where it's at."[24]

He settled on attending St. John's University, a private university located in the media capital of the world, New York City. It was there that the college student would launch his music career.

Freshman Blues

Cole found the move from Fayetteville to America's most populous city to be a bit overwhelming. "First of all, I had to get my sense of direction around here, it's such a big city," he says. "[I had to] figure out how things work as far as trains." Coming from the South, Cole experienced culture shock. "I had to adjust to attitudes," he recalls. "It's faster paced so people have much shorter tempers and just different interactions with people. So I had to get used to all of that, get adjusted to being in school and not being around any family and having that to fall back on."[25]

With all the changes in his life, Cole did not spend a lot of time on his music. "I got to school. I might have made seven beats my freshman year. Which is nothin'. That's terrible," he told Lee Hawkins of the *Wall Street Journal*. "My whole freshman year was just like an adjustment. I almost forgot that I even did music. Thankfully, I brought my beat machine, so it would remind me. But I still made seven beats that year, maybe ten, I don't know."[26]

Cole enrolled at St. John's University as a computer science major. He soon decided that computer science was not for him. He told *Interview* magazine that he had a change of heart after spending time with one of his professors. "I had this one professor who was the loneliest, saddest man I've ever known," Cole explains. "He was a programmer, and I knew that I didn't

Cole attended college in New York City (pictured) because he wanted to be in a city associated with the music industry. He soon switched his major from computer science to communications.

want to do whatever he did. So after that, I switched to Communications."[27] Although he left computer science behind, the introductory computer science classes gave him a deeper understanding of the digital tools he would use in his career as both an artist and a producer of his recordings.

Fresh Perspectives

Cole found the field of communications more to his liking. Instead of studying the language and workings of machines, he focused on the words and behavior of human beings. "I took some dope classes: Poetry, History of Music, History of Film," he says. "We watched all these movies that wound up getting nominated for Oscars, like *Slumdog Millionaire*."[28] His liberal arts education gave him a background in history, literature, and art, which shows up in his socially conscious, probing lyrics.

Classes were not the only thing that fostered Cole's intellectual growth. Various guest speakers also contributed to his knowledge and awareness of social issues. Cole was encouraged by the fact that several of these speakers were renowned African Americans. "I was inspired by, when I was in college, seeing some incredible speakers come to my school: Michael Eric Dyson, Spike Lee, Nikki Giovanni, and other poets and writers," he says. "I always loved that experience: going and sitting in an auditorium and listening to their opinions."[29]

College broadened Cole's horizons in other ways. He says that he benefited from meeting students from different parts of the country and diverse social backgrounds. "I left my city, I left town, I went to another place that I didn't know anybody. I met kids from all over and developed relationships. I learned so much more, and I grew," he says. He believes that these experiences set him apart from other rappers. "That average rap story that we know about is 'came from the hood, had to sell drugs.' I respect those stories, because these are my friends, too, and these are their stories, but I'm bringin' something else . . . and it's not likely, but it's still my story."[30] Cole admits that while he is being true to himself and his story, it would have been easier to make it as a rapper if he had come from a tougher background:

> Not to my fans, and not to the new generation of young kids, but there's an appeal, like *Scarface* is a lot of kids' favorite movie for a reason. There's an appeal about that edginess. Like, "Yo, I was in the streets, and I sold drugs." There's an appeal about that. So when you have that story, and it's real and authentic, and you can mix that with a skillful way to tell it. . . . Of course it would have been way easier for me to have my rappin' ability and my production ability and to have a story like that.[31]

WINNER
People's Choice Award
TORONTO
INTERNATIONAL FILM FESTIVAL 2008

TIME
"A BUOYANT HYMN TO LIFE,
AND A MOVIE TO CELEBRATE."
RICHARD CORLISS

Slumdog Millionaire was one of the movies Cole watched in his history of film class in college. His liberal arts education gave him a background in history, literature, and art, which shows up in his socially conscious lyrics.

WHAT DOES IT TAKE TO FIND A LOST LOVE?

A. MONEY   B. LUCK

C. SMARTS   D. DESTINY

A DANNY BOYLE FILM
slumdog millionaire

Some of the relationships Cole formed in college would last a lifetime and prove vital to his life and career. One of his best friends from St. John's University, Ibrahim Hamad, would later become his manager, his business partner, and the cofounder of his record label, Dreamville Records. Cole's freshman roommate, Adam Roy, would also become one of his business partners. And another classmate, Melissa Heholt, would eventually serve as the executive director of Cole's charity, the Dreamville Foundation.

Basketball Trials

Cole was so overwhelmed by his new surroundings and the rigors of college life that he decided not to try out for the St. John's basketball team as a freshman. But a year later, after he had settled into the college routine, he decided to give it a try. He went to tryouts as a walk-on, a player who was not recruited to play for the basketball team. After his tryout, the coaches asked him to return to the gym the next day for further evaluation. He decided against going. "In my mind, I'd have made the team," he says. "But I knew I wasn't ready for that type of commitment and that lifestyle. That was the moment where I decided that basketball was a pipe dream. It wasn't what I wanted to spend my next three or four years chasing. And that music was absolutely what I wanted to do."[32]

Cole loved basketball, however, so he joined an intramural team, playing against other St. John's students. In his junior year he joined the women's practice team, a group of male players who played against the women. "It wasn't about any type of status," says Cole's classmate Otoja Abit, "he just loved basketball enough that

"I decided that basketball was a pipe dream. It wasn't what I wanted to spend my next three or four years chasing. And that music was absolutely what I wanted to do."[32]

—J. Cole

Discovering J. Cole

Many of J. Cole's friends at St. John's University knew that rap was an interest of his, but they did not always know how serious he was about it. This included Ibrahim Hamad, the St. John's classmate who would later become Cole's manager and business partner. Hamad remembers when he discovered how talented Cole really was:

> In late 2005, 2006, Cole and I started kicking it. I didn't know he rapped like that. I saw him around school . . . just freestyling and . . . playing around, but I didn't know he was a rapper, or that [rapping] was his goal. I found out, probably in 2007, he was serious about [rapping]. I found out when I got in his car and he had a freestyle on *The Come Up* over [Kanye's] the "Grammy Family" beat. . . . He was playing it and then quickly tried to turn it off. I asked him, "Who is that?"

Cole told Hamad it was his own rap. Hamad continues, "I was like, 'Oh? You record rap? . . .' That's still one of my favorite freestyles he has ever done. . . . I was blown away."

Quoted in Yoh Phillips, "'The Warm Up' 10 Years Later: Ibrahim 'IB' Hamad Reflects on Launching J. Cole's Career," DJ Booth, June 14, 2019. https://djbooth.net.

he just wanted to play during his off time and hopefully help out the program. He competed, too. If you saw those women's practices, he was really going after the ball."[33] Cole played hard, but he was not overly aggressive, according to Monique McLean, a starter on the women's varsity team. "My freshman year, Cole would play with [the women's team] consistently," she says. "He was competitive and physical, but he'd never try to hurt us or anything like that. Sometimes guys who practice with the women's team are there just to showboat and be nasty and mean—but he was never like that. He was very nice and respectful."[34]

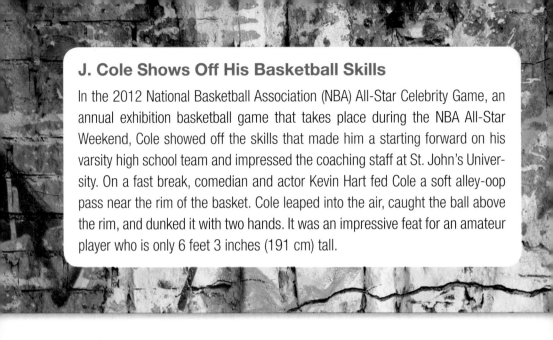

J. Cole Shows Off His Basketball Skills

In the 2012 National Basketball Association (NBA) All-Star Celebrity Game, an annual exhibition basketball game that takes place during the NBA All-Star Weekend, Cole showed off the skills that made him a starting forward on his varsity high school team and impressed the coaching staff at St. John's University. On a fast break, comedian and actor Kevin Hart fed Cole a soft alley-oop pass near the rim of the basket. Cole leaped into the air, caught the ball above the rim, and dunked it with two hands. It was an impressive feat for an amateur player who is only 6 feet 3 inches (191 cm) tall.

Back to Business

Once Cole had adjusted to college life, he returned to music. "My sophomore year is when I kinda started to remember, like, 'Okay, don't forget why you came up here, and get back to it,'" he says. He started making beats again and writing new lyrics. He spent more and more of his free time creating his music. "By my junior year, I was all the way back in, writin' songs all the time," he says. "I would walk to school or walk to class, have rhymes in my head, writin' raps in class, makin' beats at home. I got back into it and really got focused."[35]

Cole used his recording equipment to make CDs of his raps, which he sold to other students for a dollar each or sometimes just gave away. McLean remembers:

> Jermaine was really determined musically, so in the spring or anytime it was hot he would just be on the Strip [a tree-lined walkway between the residence halls and dining hall where students congregate], passing out CDs. This happened all the time. People were like, "Oh, here he goes again with the CDs." I took one because we were kind of friends. Now it's like, wow, he came a long way. I wish I still had mine.[36]

In his senior year Cole was elected president of Haraya, a pan-African student organization that gives a voice to students of color at the university. As one of his duties, Cole would introduce the musicians Haraya invited to play on campus. Not only did Cole speak to the crowd, he also performed as an opening act. He did not always receive a warm reception, according to Abit. "As always in New York City, people give you a hard time unless you're a big name," says Abit, "but you could see that he took it seriously."[37]

In 2007 Cole graduated magna cum laude with a major in communications, a minor in business, and a 3.8 grade point average. The same month that he graduated, Cole released his first

"Jermaine was really determined musically, so in the spring or anytime it was hot he would just be on the Strip, passing out CDs."[36]

—Monique McLean, a classmate of J. Cole's at St. John's University

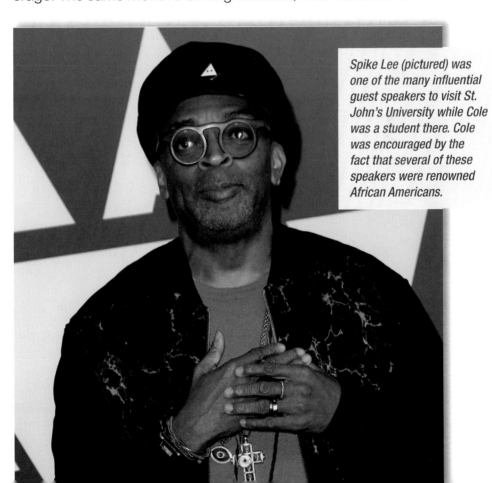

Spike Lee (pictured) was one of the many influential guest speakers to visit St. John's University while Cole was a student there. Cole was encouraged by the fact that several of these speakers were renowned African Americans.

professional mixtape, *The Come Up*. It features him rapping over his own beats as well as those he sampled from rappers Kanye West, Large Professor, and Just Blaze.

A few months after graduation, in late 2007, Cole read online that rapper and producer Jay-Z was finishing his *American Gangster* album, a work inspired by the movie of the same name. Knowing the location of Jay-Z's studio in New York, Cole decided to give a CD with two of his beats to Jay-Z for possible use on the album. Cole saw it as a way to connect with one of his idols and perhaps generate interest in his work. He waited outside the studio for two hours until Jay-Z and his entourage arrived. He describes what happened next: "He walks up to the door. I have a CD out—I took my time with this thing, I kind of decorated it, I put [it] in one of his old albums, trying to be creative. . . . And I reach out my hand like, 'Yo, Jay, here you go!' He just looked at me like, almost disgusted, like, 'I don't want that.'"[38]

Cole was crushed by the brush-off, but he learned a valuable lesson. He says, "I realized really quick, 'This is not how you're going to get on. You've got to get on through the music.'"[39] That is what he set out to do.

THE REAL WORLD

With a communications degree from St. John's University, Cole was well equipped to enter the corporate world centered in New York City. Journalism, broadcasting, public relations, advertising—all of these employment fields were open to the young graduate. But corporate communications was not his interest. Music was. "I couldn't picture myself doing anything else," he told the hip-hop news website AllHipHop. "The honest truth is I never ever even visualized any other career, I never even decided on the type of job I would look for. I knew, at least I hoped, I just knew it would be rap."[40]

Day Jobs

Without college housing to live in and with no more money coming from scholarships and student loans, Cole had to find a place to live and a job to support himself. He rented an apartment and took a job selling advertising space in a newspaper. The job paid only ten dollars an hour—a low wage for a college graduate in New York City in 2007. To make matters worse, Cole was not good at his job. In fact, he was so bad at it that a coworker put Cole's name on some of his own sales just so the rapper would not get fired.

Cole's friend Ibrahim Hamad had a better job at the *Queen Courier* newspaper and at Tritium, a now defunct bill-collection agency. Cole joined him at the latter as a bill collector, a person who calls people who are behind on credit card payments and demands payment. This job was not a good fit either. He explains:

To be good at bill-collecting, you have to ignore your feelings. I remember sitting there on the phone, listening to people tell me that they're losing their house, that their husband has cancer, and then I'm supposed to ask them if they have $50? I couldn't do that. Sometimes I would just listen to their stories and then say, "I'm sorry, have a good day." I couldn't even ask them for the money![41]

Without his boss knowing it, Cole would sometimes schedule a follow-up phone call for several months in the future, rather than a week or two later, to give the struggling family a break from the collection calls.

A Supportive Landlord

Living on his paltry income, Cole could not afford his rent. He was evicted from the first apartment he rented after graduation. Unwilling to go back to North Carolina, Cole, Hamad, and some other friends from St. John's University rented an apartment together from a man named Muhammad. Cole often fell behind in his rent there, too, but he promised to pay Muhammad once he got a recording contract. Impressed with Cole's music and determination, Muhammad never evicted him. "My landlord Muhammad he like really believed in me," Cole recalls. "So, when my rent kept piling, he never tripped. He just let me kinda just stick around."[42]

Despite working jobs he hated and being behind in his rent, Cole felt at peace with the direction his life was taking. "This is the room where it started feeling real," he says of the apartment he rented from Muhammad. "Where I started really believing and visualizing it. I used to literally wake up and tell myself like 'Yo, today I want to write a song that millions of people are gonna sing. And

> "To be good at bill-collecting, you have to ignore your feelings. . . . Sometimes I would just listen to their stories and then say, 'I'm sorry, have a good day.' I couldn't even ask them for the money!"[41]
>
> —J. Cole

millions of people gonna love.' I set that intention."[43] Once he became famous, Cole made good on his promise to Muhammad. He paid his back rent and added extra money on top of it. He also recounted Muhammad's kindness in his song "Power Trip."

Cole's friends supported the rapper's dream of musical success. "In 2007, the conversation was, we will start this label Dreamville," says Hamad. "That's how Dreamville started. We were all in Muhammad's crib. We had a house full of people that were there, and we were like, 'This will be Dreamville.' It wasn't like we had artists or any real paperwork."[44]

> "I used to literally wake up and tell myself like 'Yo, today I want to write a song that millions of people are gonna sing. And millions of people gonna love.' I set that intention."[43]
>
> —J. Cole

Constructive Criticism

All the Dreamville dreamers had was Cole, who continued to work on his music in private. Having failed to connect with Jay-Z in person, Cole was not eager to meet people in the music industry. He wanted to produce a group of recordings that would speak for itself and land him a record deal. Hamad disagreed with Cole's plan. He believed that just giving recordings to a label was not enough, no matter how good the music might be. "You're not gonna magically get signed," he told Cole. "You have to create some type of energy and get some music out."[45]

Cole realized that his friend was right. He began to work on new material with the idea of releasing another mixtape on the Internet. He did not have enough money to rent studio time in professional recording studios, but he had friends and supporters who let him in after hours to work on his music. He also began to perform live, mainly on college campuses, where he was becoming known as a talented underground rapper. His fan base was small, but it was loyal. And it was growing.

Two of J. Cole's first contacts in the music industry were rappers 50 Cent (left) and Tony Yayo (right), pictured here performing together at the Hammerstein Ballroom in New York City in 2007.

Meanwhile, Hamad started helping Cole make contacts in the music industry. They played selections from Cole's first mixtape as well as his newer songs. He and Cole met with rapper Tony Yayo and producer, DJ, and songwriter Sha Money XL at the home of recording artist 50 Cent. They met with rapper Eminem's manager, Paul Rosenberg. They also met with music executive Mark Pitts, who managed and produced some of the biggest names in the music industry, including the Notorious B.I.G, Chris Brown, and Usher. Cole and Hamad played three new songs for Pitts: "Lights Please," "Lost Ones," and "Wet Dreams." Pitts loved what he heard and offered encouragement, but several months passed without any further communication.

Belief

The wait seemed like it would never come to an end, but Cole did not let the lack of progress get him down. He kept his spirits up by telling himself over and over that he was going to succeed. Cole explains:

The only thing that can keep you going is belief—that you *know* that deal is a week away. That deal is right around the corner. It's a month away I used to tell people all the time. My mom, when I graduated college, she said: "Okay, Sweetie, what are you going to do? You graduated school." . . . But I'm like, "No, Ma, you don't know? I'm about to get a record deal in a month. I already got some things lining up." It took two years! But in my mind, there was always the belief that it was right around the corner. You almost gotta lie to yourself.[46]

The Making of "Lights Please"

Ibrahim Hamad was there when J. Cole first recorded "Lights Please," the song that brought him to the attention of Jay-Z. The recording of the first take was lost. Hamad remembers the difficulty of trying to recapture the magic of that first performance.

[Cole] did, like, 20 takes to try and get the same feeling because we lost the original file. He recorded [the original] in his bedroom so there was a particular feeling to it. When we were rerecording it, it was just me, him, and [the rapper] Mez. We started hating that song. Like. . . nothing feels right. That's when I learned no matter how much better you make it, you still think it's worse because of how long you sat with it. That went on with "Lights Please" for a while.

I remember hearing [the final version] and being blown away. No one [else] had [ever] made me feel that understanding of right where they were at; that's who he was at that time. The hook was catchy; the beat was hitting, simple yet spacious. That one was a moment of understanding, you're making songs.

Quoted in Yoh Phillips, "'The Warm Up' 10 Years Later: Ibrahim 'IB' Hamad Reflects on Launching J. Cole's Career," DJ Booth, June 14, 2019. https://djbooth.net.

Cole is quick to add that belief alone is not enough to succeed. "The talent and the hard work have to be there as well," he says. "You can't lie to yourself like, 'Man I'm about to make the [professional] league,' and you're not even on the basketball team."[47]

Buoyed by his inner confidence, Cole worked even harder to get a record deal. Instead of creating the kind of raps he loves, heavy on emotional content or social commentary, Cole tried to make songs that would be popular on radio—catchy, danceable tunes. He did this because at the time, in 2008, record companies believed that an artist had to have a radio-ready single to burst onto the scene. Without a single, there was no point in releasing an album, because no one would know about it and no one would buy it. Convinced that having a hit single was the only way to get signed, Cole moved away from his own style and tried to write songs that would appeal to music executives. Cole's team also wanted him to fit into the record company mold. "When we would go to the studio, there was almost like this pressure . . . I think we all wanted [to make] music that would get him signed," says Hamad. "We were all trying to push him to make music like . . . man, is this song going to connect with the label? That [ruined] the vibe."[48]

The pressure to create a hit song built. One night, one of the members of Cole's team offered a suggestion on how he should perform a section of a song. Cole blew up. "Don't tell me what to do," he snapped, "y'all are not the ones making this music."[49]

Cole walked out of the studio, and not just for the night. He went to the home of music producer Elite in Winchester, Connecticut, to take some time off. While he was there, he stopped thinking about radio singles and started making up freestyles. "That's where he started working on *The Warm Up*," remembers Hamad. "To him, *The Warm Up* would be freestyles." When Cole returned to New York with his new songs, Hamad was impressed with what he heard. "I don't know a hit or what will get us signed sounds like, I just know what gets me excited," he says. "I'm reacting to the freestyles like we're on to something. I can tell he's having fun. He's inspired. He's not worried about deals or being signed or whatever."[50]

Cole's Big Break

As it turned out, Cole did not need any new material to get a record contract. Without his knowledge, Mark Pitts had played "Lights Please" for his friend and associate Jay-Z, the musician who had ignored Cole outside his studio. When Pitts played "Lights Please" for Jay-Z, the rapper was in the process of launching a new record label, which he called Roc Nation. Although Jay-Z had planned to build the new label around pop artists rather than rappers, he was impressed by the newcomer's work. Pitts told Cole's team to expect a call from Jay-Z.

After trying to get Jay-Z's attention for years, Cole was reluctant to believe the good news. He was afraid of being disappointed again. But the call came through in November 2008. Cole

Rap superstar Jay-Z performs at the LG Arena in Birmingham, England, in 2010. After trying to get Jay-Z's attention for years, in 2009 Cole became the first artist signed to Jay-Z's Roc Nation record label.

J. Cole's Second Meeting with Jay-Z

In 2007 Cole tried to give Jay-Z a CD of his music, but the music mogul rebuffed him. A year later music executive Mark Pitts played Cole's "Lights Please" for Jay-Z. Impressed with what he heard, Jay-Z wanted to meet the young rapper. Cole remembers every detail of his second meeting with Jay-Z:

> I was nervous. . . . My hands were sweaty, I'm drying my hands off on my pants. I had just enough time, sitting in the waiting room to get my nerves together. He walked in . . . said what's up, sat down, got right to business. I went in there and played him a song I got called "Lights Please." Jay-Z's reactions are incredible when he's feeling [something] 'cause A. He's Jay-Z, so you're already gassed, and B. He's looking dead in your eyes, bobbing his head, intensely in the music. The best part about it is, when he's feeling something, when there's a line that he likes, he gives you that, "Wooooooo!" and he'll let you know that he's feeling it. It's a three hour meeting and we only played 5 songs, so the rest of the time, we're talking and building, you know, talking about Obama and [things]. Then three weeks later I got the confirmation text that said he wanted to do the deal. And we just went from there.

Quoted in Eddie Fu, "Knowledge Drop: How 'Lights Please' Got J. Cole Signed to Roc Nation," Genius, June 15, 2019. https://genius.com.

remembers exactly where he was when he heard from Jay-Z. He had just returned from performing at a college in California. He was feeling so good about the show that he arrived at his day job—a job he hated—early on a Monday morning. He recalls:

> I'm walking into work and I get a text like, "Yo, yo! Hit me back, you got a meeting today that you didn't know about," I'm just like . . . this is it! This is the day, this must

be it. It felt like the moment. I walked right out of work, I didn't say [anything] to nobody, dog. I didn't say what up to a manager, to another co-worker. I walked in, got the text and walked out. So about 10 minutes later I get the actual confirmation that the Jay-Z meeting is going down.[51]

Cole and Jay-Z met for about three hours. Cole played only five songs for the rap superstar. Jay-Z loved the younger man's music. They spent the rest of the meeting getting to know each other, talking about music and Cole's plans for the future.

Three weeks passed without a word from Jay-Z, but then Cole got the text that would change his life. Jay-Z offered him a recording contract. In February 2009 Cole became the first artist signed to the Roc Nation label. Cole's earlier dreams of success were finally starting to come true.

CHAPTER FOUR

STORYTELLER

When J. Cole signed with Jay-Z's record label in February 2009, he assumed that his first album would follow shortly and he would be on his way to realizing his lifelong dream of being a recording artist. He had written "Lights Please" and four other songs that Jay-Z liked. He had all the freestyle songs he had written earlier plus other new songs. Cole believed he had enough quality material to make a studio album, but Jay-Z did not agree. Like others in the music industry, Jay-Z believed that Cole needed a breakthrough single to launch his first album, and so far the young artist had not produced one.

The Warm Up

Since Jay-Z would not approve the release of an album, Cole suggested that Roc Nation release the material he had as a mixtape. The free, downloadable music would satisfy Cole's fans until a studio album was ready. Jay-Z agreed to the plan. Cole created a mixtape he called *The Warm Up*, a basketball-themed metaphor suggesting that he was getting ready to enter the music industry game.

Roc Nation released *The Warm Up* in June 2009, just four months after Cole had signed his recording contract. Featuring a captivating cover photo of Cole wearing a gray hoodie and holding a basketball while snow falls around him, the mixtape includes "Lights Please," fourteen other songs Cole had produced himself, and seven tracks recorded over beats from other producers. Robert Christgau was the only major music critic to take note of Cole's debut release. He gave *The Warm Up* a positive review in his Consumer Guide Report for MSN. Christgau recommended two songs in particular, "World Is Empty" and "Get By," but he noted missteps as well. Christgau wrote, "He's so talented you can hear how much he wants it, so talented you wince every time he shoots himself in the foot."[52] The latter comment refers to some of Cole's lyrics.

Roc Nation released "Lights Please" as a single. It was Cole's first song to enter a national chart. The song reached number nine on *Billboard*'s Bubbling Under R&B/Hip-Hop Singles chart, which tracks songs that are close to entering the main chart. However, Jay-Z's instincts about the song were right. "Lights Please" failed to break into the *Billboard* Hot 100.

Help from Jay-Z

Jay-Z's instincts were solid as well when it came to seeing Cole's potential. In August 2009 Jay-Z released the track list for his eleventh studio album, *The Blueprint 3*. Jay-Z had invited Cole to contribute a verse to the song "A Star Is Born." Cole wrote the verse in the studio in about forty-five minutes. He did not know whether his verse would be included in the final version of the song. When the track list came out, Cole was thrilled to learn that Jay-Z had used his verse and had listed him as a guest artist.

"A Star Is Born" received radio play and broke into *Billboard*'s Hot R&B/Hip-Hop Songs chart, reaching number ninety-one. The guest verse brought Cole to the attention of Jay-Z's fans. Jay-Z asked Cole to perform the verse live throughout the Jay-Z Fall Tour 2009, an eighteen-city concert tour that kicked off in New York City in September 2009. In addition to performing his verse, Cole was chosen as the opening act for the show. The tour brought Cole to the attention of even more hip-hop fans. It also brought him to the attention of booking agents at colleges. Organizations like the one Cole had been president of at St. John's University could not afford to pay a star like Jay-Z

Cole frequently attends basketball games, such as this one in North Carolina in 2017. Cole's love for the game is apparent in his 2009 mixtape, The Warm Up, which includes a cover photo of him holding a basketball.

to give a concert, but they could afford a newcomer like Cole. When Jay-Z's tour ended in November 2009, Cole stayed on the road for much of the next year, performing college gigs.

In May 2010, while still on tour, Cole released his second single, "Who Dat." The song received radio play and broke onto three *Billboard* charts, including the Hot 100. Although the song charted, it was not a major hit, and Jay-Z refused to give the go-ahead for Cole's first studio album. However, Cole received good news in August 2010. He was named Artist of the Year at the Urban Music Awards on the strength of *The Warm Up* and "Who Dat."

Friday Night Lights

Cole continued to write and produce new songs, but none met Jay-Z's standards for launching an album. Rather than discard the tracks, Cole released the best of them on his third mixtape, *Friday Night Lights*. Released in November 2010, the mixtape was streamed over 2 million times and downloaded over 1 million times on mixtape site DatPiff.

The critics reacted well to Cole's new work. AllHipHop gave the mixtape a rare ten-out-of-ten rating, commenting: "*Friday Night Lights* features 20 tracks of Hip Hop in its purest form. Pleasing every fan from purists to mainstream."[53] Writing for the online music magazine *Pitchfork*, Tom Breihan said that the mixtape "has an organic warmth that lends it an immediate approachability." Breihan praised Cole's thoughtful lyrics, writing, "Cole, who left Fayetteville for college in New York City, explores bits of his own story that little rap music has found space to address—like being the one college kid who made it out, then returning home to realize that many of his old friends are in prison or Iraq." However, Breihan also saw a problem with Cole's intellectual approach. "Cole . . . is the honor student who overthinks everything," wrote Breihan. "Each boast or proposition comes with some sort of tortured justification. It's not enough for him to enjoy the spoils of his success; he has to spell out to us that he's doing it for everyone else who grew up poor in Fayetteville, North Carolina."[54] *Friday Night Lights* received an award for best mixtape at the 2011 BET (Black Entertainment Television) Hip Hop Awards. Cole's work topped mixtapes by several soon-to-be major stars, including Big K.R.I.T.'s *Return of 4Eva*, B.o.B.'s *No Genre*, Kendrick Lamar's *Section.80*, and Frank Ocean's *Nostalgia, Ultra*. Cole was building a reputation as a serious rap artist who set his own direction, rather than following trends.

> "Cole, who left Fayetteville for college in New York City, explores bits of his own story that little rap music has found space to address."[54]
>
> —Tom Breihan, music critic for *Pitchfork*

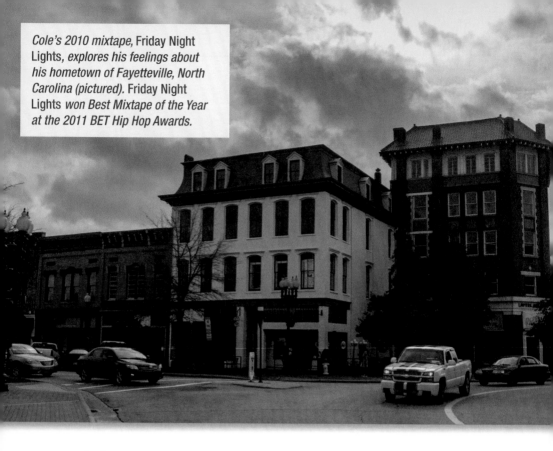

Cole's 2010 mixtape, Friday Night Lights, *explores his feelings about his hometown of Fayetteville, North Carolina (pictured).* Friday Night Lights *won Best Mixtape of the Year at the 2011 BET Hip Hop Awards.*

A Surprising Debut

Cole continued touring throughout 2010 and 2011. Nearly three years had passed since he had first played his songs for Jay-Z. His mixtapes had earned solid reviews from critics. His singles had charted. And he had won awards for his music. Hip-hop fans and industry insiders were wondering when, if ever, the young rapper would release a studio album. Although Cole still had not had a blockbuster single, Jay-Z finally approved the release of his debut album. Cole called it *Cole World: The Sideline Story*. The title, another basketball metaphor, refers to the fact that Cole created the album's tracks while still on the sidelines of the music industry, waiting to get into the game.

Roc Nation released *Cole World: The Sideline Story* in September 2011. No one—not even Cole—was ready for what happened next. Jay-Z and the other executives at Roc Nation expected the album to sell about 60,000 copies the first week. Instead, it sold a whopping 218,000 copies, launching it to number one on the *Billboard* 200 album chart. Although Cole did not expect to sell that many copies the first week, he did think Roc Nation's estimate of 60,000 copies was low. He based his assessment on the fact that his live concerts had been selling out for nearly two years and he was being recognized everywhere he went.

The album got mixed reviews. Brad Wete of *Entertainment Weekly* praised it. He wrote, "*Cole World: The Sideline Story* is a well-rounded effort, and deeper than most, offering cuts that tackle unplanned pregnancy ('Lost Ones') and uncertain love ('Nobody's Perfect')."[55] Jody Rosen of *Rolling Stone* called Cole "a technically superb rapper, packing these sleek, snappy, mostly self-produced tracks with dozens of great punch lines," but he was less impressed with Cole's handling of emotional topics. He wrote, "While he tries to wring pathos out of everything from career struggles to unplanned pregnancies, the melodrama feels rote; the rhymes hit the mark but the stories leave you cold."[56] Jayson Greene of *Pitchfork* was even less impressed. "People appear to care deeply about this guy," Greene wrote. "But it's difficult to imagine why from the evidence of this studiously bland and compromise-riddled record, which seems to be searching for the meeting point of every conceivable middle."[57]

A Music Video Creates Controversy

To support the single "Who Dat," J. Cole made a music video in his hometown of Fayetteville, North Carolina. The video, which aired in 2010, features Cole performing the song as he walks through the city surrounded by cheerleaders from Fayetteville State University and the E.E. Smith High School marching band. The video proved controversial. The university and the local school board objected to having their schools associated with the song's profanity and explicit lyrics. Cumberland County School Superintendent Frank Till said the school district did not allow students to use that kind of language at school, and it made no sense to have them performing in a video that featured it. Till tried—and failed—to get the song pulled from YouTube and other video platforms.

Sophomore Jinx

A recording artist's second album, often referred to as his or her sophomore album, is always a big test. The history of popular music is filled with stories of artists whose first albums were hits but whose second albums flopped. This is known as the sophomore jinx. The jinx is a particular danger for artists who write their own material. They often use their best songs to break into the industry, but then they do not have follow-up material of equal quality. Some critics felt that Cole's second album, *Born Sinner*, suffered from the sophomore jinx.

Released in June 2013, *Born Sinner* sold well initially but did not go on to sell as well as *Cole World: The Sideline Story*. *Pitchfork*'s Corban Goble believed that Cole had shown little or no artistic progress since the release of *Cole World*. Goble wrote: "Cole's second, attention-grabbing mixtape, 2009's *The Warm Up*, positioned him as an upstart unmoored from traditional conventions, an artist who could switch up flows, rap furiously and build his own hooks; *Born Sinner* finds him standing in about the same place he was on *Cole World: The Sideline Story*." Several critics wondered aloud if Cole would ever live up to the potential that Jay-Z had seen in him. "Several releases deep into Cole's growing catalogue, we haven't been delivered the savior that Jay-Z's 'A Star is Born' seemed to anoint,"[58] wrote Goble.

Hitting His Stride

Cole silenced the doubters with his third album, *2014 Forest Hills Drive*. Named for the address of Cole's childhood home in Fayetteville, the album comments on the artist's struggles growing up, the challenges he faced when he moved from North Carolina to New York City, and the difficulties of breaking into the music industry. As usual, Cole produced most of the tracks, and this album featured no guest artists. Announced only three weeks before its December 2014 release, and without any singles leading into it, *2014 Forest Hills Drive* sold an incredible 371,000 copies in its first week. The album rose to number one on the *Billboard*

200, making Cole one of just six rappers to reach number one with their first three albums. The album also shattered One Direction's record for most album streams on Spotify, being streamed over 15.7 million times in its first week, compared to One Direction's 11.5 million. To date, *2014 Forest Hills Drive* remains Cole's best-selling album, with more than 1.2 million copies sold.

Most critics were impressed with *2014 Forest Hills Drive*. "J. Cole's determined to make music that matters to *him*. He shines without any features, standing strong in his delivery and carrying his story to the forefront of the 13-track project," wrote Erin

Cole Receives a 360 Deal

When J. Cole received a recording contract from Jay-Z's record label, Roc Nation, the young rapper eagerly signed it. Later, however, he expressed dissatisfaction with the contract, mainly because it was what is known as a 360 deal. A 360 contract is different from the contracts that used to be standard in the recording industry. Under non-360 contracts, the record label profits only from the sales of the recordings it has released into the market. The artists are paid a royalty from their recordings, but they make most of their money by playing concerts (and from the sale of T-shirts and other merchandise).

With a 360 deal, the record label receives a portion of everything the artist earns from concerts, merchandising, and even music publishing. In an interview with the online youth culture website Complex, Cole says that he does not like the fact that a portion of his concert and merchandise earnings goes to the record company. However, he admits that 360 deals can benefit an artist whose recordings are not selling well. Under the old system, when record companies only made money from record sales, a label would drop an artist whose records were not selling. But with a 360 deal, a label can still earn money by sending the artist on tour. This keeps the label happy and allows the artist to continue releasing recordings.

Lowers of Exclaim! "He has definitely graduated into a class of his own."[59] *2014 Forest Hills Drive* was nominated for the 2016 Grammy award for Best Rap Album, and in 2015 it won Album of the Year at the BET Hip Hop Awards and Rap Album of the Year at the *Billboard* Music Awards.

A Change of Direction

Cole's fourth studio album, *4 Your Eyez Only*, was released just before Christmas 2016 and also debuted at number one. The album marked a departure for Cole. *4 Your Eyez Only* is not based on Cole's life. Instead, it is a concept album that tells the story of a young man as he goes from selling crack to falling in love and becoming a father. The last track reveals that the young father has died and the album is a tape he created for his daughter to listen to after his death. Cole uses the story to explore concerns in the African American community, including mass incarceration, racial discrimination, gang violence, and depression. Music critic Craig Jenkins of *New York* magazine called *4 Your Eyez Only* Cole's "best and most mature album."[60]

> "J. Cole's determined to make music that matters to *him*. He shines without any features, standing strong in his delivery and carrying his story to the forefront of the 13-track project."[59]
>
> —Erin Lowers, music critic for Exclaim!

Cole followed up the concept album with another strongly themed work, *KOD*, which he explains stands for three things: Kids on Drugs, King Overdose, and Kill Our Demons. He elaborates that King Overdose refers to himself and Kill Our Demons refers to breaking free of past trauma. Released in April 2018, *KOD* was Cole's fifth consecutive album to reach number one on the *Billboard* 200, selling 397,000 album-equivalent units in its first week to debut at the top of the charts. It also debuted at number one in Australia, Canada, Ireland, and New Zealand. On the first day of its release, *KOD* broke streaming records on both Spotify and Apple Music, with a total of 64.5 million streams on Apple Music, breaking the previous record for *Views* by Drake in 2017. The only guest artist appearing on the album was kiLL Edward, which is a pseudonym for Cole himself. The album solidified Cole's reputation as his generation's most serious and socially aware rapper.

CHAPTER FIVE

GIVING BACK

J. Cole made the *Forbes* list of the one hundred highest-earning celebrities in 2018. *Forbes* estimated that Cole earned $35.5 million before taxes and expenses that year. While some of that income came from his records, most of it came from Cole's tour dates, which earned Cole more than $1 million per concert. Cole dropped off the list in 2019, but he is still a wealthy man. However, he says he does not love money, only the security it provides. And while he spends some of his money on things he enjoys, he also donates some of it to those who are less fortunate than he is.

Dreamville Foundation

In October 2011 Cole founded Dreamville Foundation, a nonprofit organization with the goal of helping provide better futures for urban youth in Fayetteville, North Carolina. The foundation's Facebook page describes how Cole's life experience was the driving force behind the organization's mission:

Recording artist J. Cole established the Dreamville Foundation in October 2011 to uplift the urban youth of Fayetteville, North Carolina by bridging the gap between them and the world of opportunities that are available. After moving to New York City to attend college, J. Cole realized the world has so much to offer beyond the borders of his hometown, Fayetteville. He strives to make the youth of Fayetteville aware of their potential and opportunities through promoting education and creating programs and events that will allow our youth to be "Set up for Success." At an early age J. Cole knew he wanted to be a rapper, and through his foundation he encourages urban youth to have dreams, believe in their dreams, and achieve their dreams.[61]

Dreamville Foundation sponsors two annual programs: the Back to School Supply Giveaway and the Annual Dreamville Weekend. The Back to School Supply Giveaway provides Fayetteville students with the tools and supplies they need to have a successful school year, including binders, folders, backpacks, and clothing. The Annual Dreamville Weekend hosts a series of events that provide youths with the chance to make connections with people who can help them pursue their dreams. Events include an Appreciation Dinner that recognizes community leaders and outstanding students. The foundation also hosts a Career Day panel of African American professionals representing a range of occupations and industries. The idea is to let urban youth know that there are many more career opportunities than they might expect. "I want to start the process of showing them there are other options besides what's on the [television] screen," says Cole. "They don't have to be a rapper or an athlete; there are people who manage the rappers, who book the shows. There are so many jobs you can do; this is about expanding their minds to those possibilities."[62]

> "I want to start the process of showing them there are other options besides what's on the [television] screen. They don't have to be a rapper or an athlete."[62]
>
> —J. Cole

Wide-Ranging Community Support

While the Annual Dreamville Weekend is a major endeavor, the Dreamville Foundation is busy throughout the year. It provides assistance to the community in many ways. For example, it sponsors a book club, in which participants read and discuss books, fostering a love and appreciation for the written word. It also works in the areas of low-cost housing, cultural celebration, and disaster relief.

The Dreamville Foundation provides permanent low-cost housing for single-parent households. In 2014 Cole purchased his childhood home at 2014 Forest Hills Drive in Fayetteville for $120,000 through the Dreamville Foundation. Cole upgraded the home, which had been repossessed from his mother years earlier, to turn it into rent-free accommodations for needy families. "It'll be a place somebody can come and live rent-free, two or three years at a time," Cole explains. "I'm imagining a single mother, who can hopefully leave in a better position than when they came."[63]

To help raise funds for the Dreamville Foundation Cole had planned to sponsor a festival in Fayetteville in September 2018.

The Back to School Supply Giveaway, part of Cole's Dreamville Foundation, provides Fayetteville, North Carolina, students with binders, folders, backpacks, and clothing to help them succeed in school.

Cole on Marriage and Family

In 2018 J. Cole gave an interview to Paul Cantor of the website Vulture that covered topics the rapper had never addressed before, including his life away from the spotlight. In this excerpt, he discusses the importance of marriage and parenthood:

> I'm a . . . successful rapper, who can literally at the drop of a hat go anywhere, do anything, have mad adventures. . . . But there was no better decision I could have made than the discipline I put on myself of having responsibility, having another human being—my wife—that I have to answer to. Family can literally be the thing you always needed, bring balance and meaning and fuel your creativity, give you purpose.
>
> [Comedian and actor] Dave Chappelle gave me some baby advice. . . . He said: You'll hit another gear, you'll hit a gear that you never knew you had when you have kids. It actually proved to be true.

Quoted in Paul Cantor, "J. Cole Just Wants to Be Himself," Vulture, April 25, 2018. www.vulture.com.

The Dreamville Festival was intended to feature local music, culture, food, and art. Wanting to help young rappers the way that Jay-Z had helped him, Cole said the entertainment lineup would include a mix of up-and-comers and national acts. In addition to Cole, headliners were to include SZA, Big Sean, Young Thug, and Nelly. However, Hurricane Florence struck North Carolina in the week prior to the festival, so Cole postponed it. The festival, attended by a sellout crowd of more than forty thousand people, finally took place in April 2019.

The rescheduling of the festival was the least of the problems caused by Hurricane Florence. It devastated the communities across North Carolina. In September 2018 the storm dumped a record-breaking 30 inches (76.2 cm) of rainfall on the state,

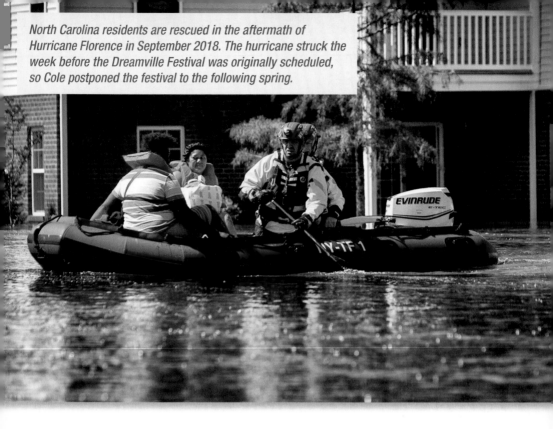

North Carolina residents are rescued in the aftermath of Hurricane Florence in September 2018. The hurricane struck the week before the Dreamville Festival was originally scheduled, so Cole postponed the festival to the following spring.

causing widespread flooding. More than nineteen thousand people were forced out of their homes from the effects of the hurricane. The Dreamville Foundation provided affected residents with hot food stations placed throughout Fayetteville. It identified temporary housing options for families, set up food pantries, and created emergency shelters. It also provided financial support to other nonprofits that provided services for local residents.

Music Executive

In addition to his nonprofit activities, Cole is also involved in business endeavors. The music industry attention that came his way when he was signed to Jay-Z's Roc Nation is an experience Cole wants to share with other young artists. With that in mind, he cofounded Dreamville Records with his friend and associate Ibrahim Hamad. In addition to Cole, the label has a stable of eleven recording artists who have released more than thirty albums, mixtapes, and extended-play singles. The label has also released several short documentary and live concert films.

One of the label's biggest successes to date is *Revenge of the Dreamers III*, a compilation album that was released in July 2019. The album features twenty-seven producers and thirty-four artists, including Dreamville talents Bas, Cozz, Omen, Lute, Ari Lennox, EarthGang, J.I.D., and J. Cole. Cole announced the album on Twitter, writing, "Revenge album dropping 2nite. Know that this album represents community and the unheard unsung artist that fight and bleed daily to be felt. There will be someone you never heard of on this album. Look them up and support them if they resonate with you. A follow goes a long way."[64] A few minutes later, he added, "Same goes for the producers that go unheard and make beats all day every day hoping to cut through. To the producers and artists that came through but didn't make the album, you are there in spirit. Thank you for your presence, the energy of those sessions was the most magical."[65]

Revenge of the Dreamers III sold 115,000 units in its first week, making it number one on the *Billboard* 200 album chart. It was Cole's sixth consecutive number one album. Cole cowrote eight of the album's eighteen tracks and appears as a guest artist on seven of them. He performs the eighth song, "Middle Child," by himself. Released as a single in January 2019, "Middle Child" went to number one on the *Billboard* Rhythmic chart, to number two on the Hot R&B/Hip-Hop Songs chart, and to number four on the *Billboard* Hot 100 chart, making it the highest-charting song of Cole's career.

Critics praised *Revenge of the Dreamers III*. Sheldon Pearce of *Pitchfork* called the work a "successful meeting of the minds."[66] Lucy Shanker of the online magazine *Consequence of Sound* credits Cole for helping the younger artists on his label without using them to further his own career. "If Cole's greater purpose was boosting the career of his prodigies, he succeeded," Shanker writes. "Instead of being a fan of artists whose talent reaches in different directions than his and subsequently exploiting their sound for his own benefit, Cole has provided the ultimate platform for underground artists to succeed."[67]

> "Cole has provided the ultimate platform for underground artists to succeed."[67]
>
> —Lucy Shanker, music critic for Consequence of Sound

J. Cole Visits the White House

Because of the social awareness J. Cole displays in his music and the actions he has taken to help disadvantaged members of his community, President Barack Obama invited him to the White House in April 2016 to discuss prison reform. Cole joined several other singers and rappers known for their work in the African American community. Among them were singer Alicia Keys, who has lobbied Congress to pass criminal justice reform legislation; Chance the Rapper, who leads an antiviolence campaign in Chicago; and Common, Wale, and Ludacris, who, like Cole, support youth programs. The group discussed the president's My Brother's Keeper initiative, a partnership of private organizations and the US government that encourages civic leaders to engage with young men of color to address their challenges and to promote racial justice.

Cole later turned this experience into a rap that he called "High for Hours." In the 2017 rap, he describes a conversation with the president about the struggles of African Americans. Cole uses his song to urge Obama to find ways to fix those problems.

Mitch Findlay of *HotNewHipHop*, an online magazine and music sharing platform, singled out Cole's contributions as the high points of *Revenge of the Dreamers III*. Findlay writes:

It's no surprise that J. Cole is the first artist we hear, a move emblematic of his role as the grand orchestrator. As expected, Cole is in fine form throughout, lyrically focused and ably flitting between a veteran presence and a marquee player. At 34, it feels as if Cole has only now entered his prime. "Sunset," which features the unexpected pairing of J. Cole and Young Nudy, finds the former sliding through a welcome sense of aloof swagger. . . . Though "Sacrifices" features excellent performances from Johnny Venus, Smino, and Saba, Cole's climactic verse seems destined to stand as one of his greatest yet; it's not easy to inject sincere emotion into technically sound bars, but Cole appears to have reached new levels of artistry.[68]

One of the songs on *Revenge of the Dreamers III* contains an interesting clue about Cole's private life. In a January 2016 interview, Cole revealed that he was married to Melissa Heholt, a former classmate of his at St. John's University, whom he had been dating for ten years. A teacher and an entrepreneur, Heholt had founded a successful event-planning business called Statice in

Cole performs onstage during Summerfest in Milwaukee, Wisconsin, in 2018. That year Forbes put Cole on its list of the one hundred highest-earning celebrities, estimating his earnings for the year at $35.5 million.

New York. She later became the executive director of the Dreamville Foundation. In a May 2018 interview with radio host Angie Martinez, Cole stated that he and Heholt have a son together. In the song "Sacrifices" on *Revenge of the Dreamers III*, Cole raps a lyric revealing that he and Heholt are expecting another child.

The same day that Dreamville Records released "Middle Child," it announced that Cole would release his sixth solo album in 2019. The official announcement followed a hint that Cole gave on his *KOD* album. The album's last track, "1985," bears the subtitle "Intro to *The Fall Off*," suggesting that *The Fall Off* would be the title of Cole's next album. In "1985" Cole says that he has always been on a quest to create the next wave in hip-hop music. Many critics consider "1985" to be the best track on *KOD*. Based on that song, many critics believe that *The Fall Off* could be another step forward for Cole.

Poised for Even Greater Success

Cole has taken an unusual path to the top of the rap world, attending college, graduating with honors, and slowly building a fan base without the benefit of chart-topping singles. He patiently waited for almost three years after signing a recording contract to have his first album released. It is a path that might have discouraged many artists, but Cole kept going, releasing albums that he produced and performed by himself, shunning guest artists and other gimmicks to sell records.

His progress has been slow and filled with life lessons. When success finally came, he was well grounded, a fact that has helped him avoid the self-destructive lifestyle that has engulfed so many recording stars. Cole's social commentary and personal reflections give his music substance, and he has the artistic restlessness to approach his themes from fresh directions, assuming the voices of characters who are different from him. Now married and a father, having gained financial security for himself and his family, Cole is free to move in any direction he wants as an artist. Critics hope and his fans believe that his greatest work is ahead of him.

Introduction: Voice of the Community

1. Quoted in Jamilah King, "J. Cole Talks About Colorism in Hip-Hop and the White House," Colorlines, August 22, 2013. www.colorlines.com.
2. Quoted in Jordan Darville, "J. Cole Talks Kendrick Collab, Kanye West, and kiLL Edward in New Interview," Fader, May 16, 2018. www.thefader.com.
3. Sam Moore, "J. Cole—'KOD' Review," New Musical Express, April 24, 2018. www.nme.com.

Chapter One: Academic Achiever

4. Quoted in Guy Raz, "J. Cole: An Upstart Rapper Speaks for Himself," NPR, November 1, 2011. www.npr.org.
5. Quoted in David Smyth, "The Gentle Rapper: J Cole Interview," Evening Standard (London), December 9, 2014. www.standard.co.uk.
6. Quoted in Smyth, "The Gentle Rapper."
7. Quoted in Raz, "J. Cole."
8. Quoted in King, "J. Cole Talks About Colorism in Hip-Hop and the White House."
9. Quoted in King, "J. Cole Talks About Colorism in Hip-Hop and the White House."
10. Quoted in Raz, "J. Cole."
11. Quoted in Raz, "J. Cole."
12. Quoted in Bryan Armen Graham, "J. Cole on His Hoop Dreams, and Why the World Won't Allow LeBron to Be as Great as MJ," Sports Illustrated, June 12, 2013. www.si.com.
13. Quoted in Graham, "J. Cole on His Hoop Dreams, and Why the World Won't Allow LeBron to Be as Great as MJ."
14. Quoted in Graham, "J. Cole on His Hoop Dreams, and Why the World Won't Allow LeBron to Be as Great as MJ."
15. Quoted in Graham, "J. Cole on His Hoop Dreams, and Why the World Won't Allow LeBron to Be as Great as MJ."
16. Quoted in Shane Ryu, "8 Years of Beats: Inside J. Cole's Unsung Career as a Producer," Central Sauce, January 8, 2019. https://centralsauce.com.

17. Quoted in Steve Lobel, "J Cole Talks Tupac, Jay Z, Eminem & Dreamville Live with Steve Lobel," YouTube, September 30, 2014. https://youtu.be/5CvED0F5LAw.

18. Quoted in Lobel, "J Cole Talks Tupac, Jay Z, Eminem & Dreamville Live with Steve Lobel."

19. Quoted in Complex, "J. Cole Talks Roc Nation, Meeting Jay-Z & 'The Warm Up' Mixtape," May 2, 2009. www.complex .com.

20. Quoted in Ryu, "8 Years of Beats."

21. Quoted in Rap-Up, "J. Cole Reminisces on MTV's 'When I Was 17,'" November 12, 2011. www.rap-up.com.

22. Quoted in Ryu, "8 Years of Beats."

23. Quoted in Henna Kathiya, "J. Cole's Rap Name Was 'Therapist,' on 'When I Was 17,'" MTV News, November 11, 2011. www.mtv.com.

Chapter Two: Communications Major

24. Quoted in *Wall Street Journal*, "Rapper J. Cole Talks for Nearly an Hour to the *WSJ*'s Lee Hawkins—J. Cole Interview," YouTube, August 14, 2013. https://youtu.be/GZ1NW_ZjBz4.

25. Quoted in AllHipHop Staff, "J. Cole: Roc Nation's Young Gun," AllHipHop, June 15, 2009. https://allhiphop.com.

26. Quoted in *Wall Street Journal*, "Rapper J. Cole Talks for Nearly an Hour to the *WSJ*'s Lee Hawkins—J. Cole Interview."

27. Quoted in David Shapiro, "J. Cole's Tales Out of School," *Interview*, February 4, 2013. www.interviewmagazine.com.

28. Quoted in Shapiro, "J. Cole's Tales Out of School."

29. Quoted in Shapiro, "J. Cole's Tales Out of School."

30. Quoted in *Wall Street Journal*, "Rapper J. Cole Talks for Nearly an Hour to the *WSJ*'s Lee Hawkins—J. Cole Interview."

31. Quoted in *Wall Street Journal*, "Rapper J. Cole Talks for Nearly an Hour to the *WSJ*'s Lee Hawkins—J. Cole Interview."

32. Quoted in Natalie Weiner, "The Oral History of J. Cole's Basketball Career," Bleacher Report, April 19, 2017. https:// bleacherreport.com.

33. Quoted in Weiner, "The Oral History of J. Cole's Basketball Career."

34. Quoted in Weiner, "The Oral History of J. Cole's Basketball Career."

35. Quoted in *Wall Street Journal*, "Rapper J. Cole Talks for Nearly an Hour to the *WSJ*'s Lee Hawkins—J. Cole Interview."
36. Quoted in Weiner, "The Oral History of J. Cole's Basketball Career."
37. Quoted in Weiner, "The Oral History of J. Cole's Basketball Career."
38. Quoted in Raz, "J. Cole."
39. Quoted in Raz, "J. Cole."

Chapter Three: The Real World
40. Quoted in AllHipHop Staff, "J. Cole."
41. Quoted in Shapiro, "J. Cole's Tales Out of School."
42. Quoted in Danielle Harling, "J. Cole Recalls Troubles Paying Rent, Says He's an Underdog," HipHopDX, October 24, 2013. https://hiphopdx.com.
43. Quoted in Harling, "J. Cole Recalls Troubles Paying Rent, Says He's an Underdog."
44. Quoted in Yoh Phillips, "'The Warm Up' 10 Years Later: Ibrahim 'IB' Hamad Reflects on Launching J. Cole's Career," DJ Booth, June 14, 2019. https://djbooth.net.
45. Quoted in Phillips, "'The Warm Up' 10 Years Later."
46. Quoted in *Wall Street Journal*, "Rapper J. Cole Talks for Nearly an Hour to the *WSJ*'s Lee Hawkins—J. Cole Interview."
47. Quoted in *Wall Street Journal*, "Rapper J. Cole Talks for Nearly an Hour to the *WSJ*'s Lee Hawkins—J. Cole Interview."
48. Quoted in Phillips, "'The Warm Up' 10 Years Later."
49. Quoted in Phillips, "'The Warm Up' 10 Years Later."
50. Quoted in Phillips, "'The Warm Up' 10 Years Later."
51. Quoted in Complex, "J. Cole Talks Roc Nation, Meeting Jay-Z & 'The Warm Up' Mixtape."

Chapter Four: Storyteller
52. Robert Christgau, "J Cole," Robert Christgau (website), 2009. www.robertchristgau.com.
53. AlllHipHop Staff, "Review: J. Cole—*Friday Night Lights*," AllHipHop, November 15, 2010. https://allhiphop.com.
54. Tom Breihan, "J. Cole *Friday Night Lights*," *Pitchfork*, November 29, 2010. https://pitchfork.com.
55. Brad Wete, "*Cole World: The Sideline Story* Review—J. Cole," *Entertainment Weekly*, September 22, 2011. https://ew.com.

56. Jody Rosen, *"Cole World: The Sideline Story,"* *Rolling Stone*, September 27, 2011. www.rollingstone.com.

57. Jayson Greene, *"Cole World: The Sideline Story,"* *Pitchfork*, September 30, 2011. https://pitchfork.com.

58. Corban Goble, *"Born Sinner,"* *Pitchfork*, June 21, 2013. https://pitchfork.com.

59. Erin Lowers, "J. Cole *2014 Forest Hills Drive*," Exclaim!, December 9, 2014. http://exclaim.ca.

60. Craig Jenkins, "J. Cole's *4 Your Eyez Only* Is His Best and Most Mature Album," Vulture, December 15, 2016. www .vulture.com.

Chapter Five: Giving Back

61. Dreamville Foundation, "Company Overview," Facebook, 2011. www.facebook.com.

62. Quoted in Jamie Isaacs, "J. Cole Is More than Just a Rapper," Odyssey, July 4, 2016. www.theodysseyonline.com.

63. Quoted in Smyth, "The Gentle Rapper."

64. J. Cole (@JColeNC), "Revenge album dropping 2nite," Twitter, July 5, 2019, 5:59 a.m. https://twitter.com.

65. J. Cole (@JColeNC), "Same goes for the producers that go unheard and make beats all day every day hoping to cut through," Twitter, July 5, 2019, 6:04 a.m. https://twitter.com.

66. Sheldon Pearce, "Various Artists *Revenge of the Dreamers III*," *Pitchfork*, July 9, 2019. https://pitchfork.com.

67. Lucy Shanker, "Dreamville and J. Cole Present a Scattered View of the Hip-Hop Landscape on *Revenge of the Dreamers III*," Consequence of Sound, July 12, 2019. https://consequenceofsound.net.

68. Mitch Findlay, "Dreamville 'Revenge of the Dreamers 3' Review," HotNewHipHop, July 10, 2019. www.hotnewhiphop .com.

Important Events in the Life of J. Cole

1985

Jermaine Lamarr Cole is born on January 28, 1985, at the US Army Ninety-Seventh General Hospital, Frankfurt, West Germany.

1993

Cole hears Tupac Shakur's album *2Pacalypse Now* and is moved by the music.

1997

Inspired by his cousin's freestyle rapping, Cole tries rapping and falls in love with it.

2000

Cole's mother gives him a music sampler and drum machine for Christmas.

2001

Cole begins posting his songs on Internet forums using the stage name Blaza.

2002

Cole joins local rap group Bomm Sheltuh as a rapper and a producer.

2003

Cole graduates from Terry Sanford High School and enrolls at St. John's University.

2007

Cole graduates magna cum laude from St. John's University.

2008

Cole meets with Jay-Z, who offers him a recording contract.

2009

Roc Nation releases Cole's second mixtape, *The Warm Up*.

2010
Cole releases his third mixtape, *Friday Night Lights*.

2011
Cole's first album, *Cole World: The Sideline Story*, debuts at number one on the *Billboard* 200 album chart.

2012
Cole is nominated for Best New Artist for the 2012 Grammy Awards.

2013
Cole releases his second studio album, *Born Sinner*.

2014
Cole releases his third studio album, *2014 Forest Hills Drive*, which debuts at number one on the *Billboard* 200.

2015
2014 Forest Hills Drive wins Album of the Year at the BET Hip Hop Awards and Rap Album of the Year at the *Billboard* Music Awards.

2016
Cole releases his fourth studio album, the concept album *4 Your Eyez Only*.

2018
Cole releases his fifth consecutive number one album, *KOD*.

2019
Dreamville Records releases *Revenge of the Dreamers III*, a compilation album featuring thirty-four artists, including J. Cole, who cowrote and performs on eight songs.

Books

Judy Dodge Cummings, *Men of Hip-Hop*. Minneapolis: ABDO, 2017.

Stuart A. Kallen, *Rap and Hip-Hop*. San Diego: Reference-Point, 2020.

Alicia Z. Klepeis, *J. Cole: Chart-Topping Rapper*. Minneapolis: Essential Library, 2018.

Marcia Amidon Lusted, *Hip-Hop Music*. Minneapolis: ABDO, 2018.

Vanessa Oswald, *Hip-Hop: A Cultural and Musical Revolution*. New York: Lucent, 2019.

Internet Sources

Paul Cantor, "J. Cole Just Wants to Be Himself," Vulture, April 25, 2018. www.vulture.com.

Jon Caramanica, "J. Cole, the Platinum Rap Dissident, Steps Back from the Spotlight," *New York Times*, April 24, 2017. www.nytimes.com.

Jordan Darville, "J. Cole Talks Kendrick Collab, Kanye West, and kiLL Edward in New Interview," Fader, May 16, 2018. www.thefader.com.

Dee Lockett, "J. Cole Speaks Out on Cancel Culture, the Trouble with Fame, and Schooling Young Rappers," *Billboard*, September 27, 2018. www.billboard.com.

Yoh Phillips, "'The Warm Up' 10 Years Later: Ibrahim 'IB' Hamad Reflects on Launching J. Cole's Career," DJ Booth, June 14, 2019. https://djbooth.net.

Shane Ryu, "8 Years of Beats: Inside J. Cole's Unsung Career as a Producer," Central Sauce, January 8, 2019. https://centralsauce.com.

Eric Skelton, "Experiencing Dreamville's Rap Camp Through the Lens of Chase Fade," Complex, January 11, 2019. www.complex.com.

FOR MORE INFORMATION